Racing to the West

Program Consultants

Stephanie Abraham Hirsh, Ph.D.
Associate Director
National Staff Development Council
Dallas, Texas

Louise Matteoni, Ph.D.
Professor of Education
Brooklyn College
City University of New York

Karen Tindel Wiggins
Social Studies Consultant
Richardson Independent School District
Richardson, Texas

Renee Levitt
Educational Consultant
Scarsdale, New York

STECK-VAUGHN®
C O M P A N Y
ELEMENTARY • SECONDARY • ADULT • LIBRARY

MOMENTS IN AMERICAN HISTORY

Racing to the West

BY
Melissa Stone

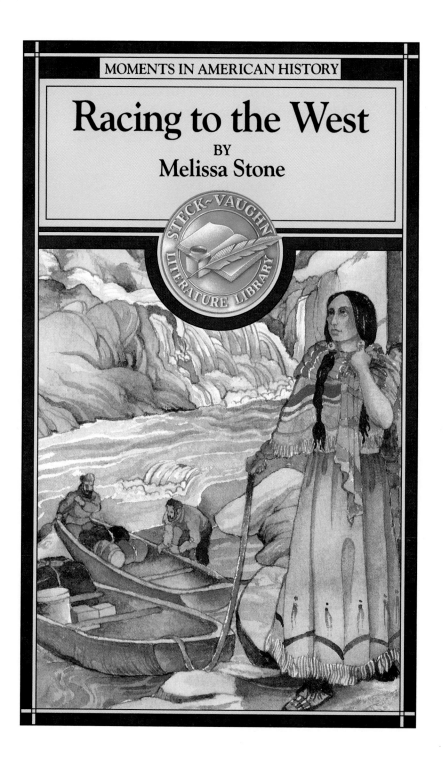

Steck-Vaughn Literature Library
Moments in American History

RISKING IT ALL
REBELLION'S SONG
CREATIVE DAYS
RACING TO THE WEST
YOU DON'T OWN ME!
CLOUDS OF WAR
A CRY FOR ACTION
LARGER THAN LIFE
FLYING HIGH
BRIGHTER TOMORROWS

Illustrations: Steve Cieslawski: 8-9, 11, 12-13, 14, 16, 19; Arvis Stewart: cover art, 20-21, 22, 24, 26, 29, 31; Rae Ecklund: 32-33, 34, 37, 39, 40, 43; Susan Lexa: 44-45, 46, 49, 51, 52, 55; Jill Kastner: 56-57, 59, 60, 63, 65, 67; Donald Cook: 68-69, 70, 73, 74, 77, 79.

Project Editor: Anne Souby

Design: Kirchoff/Wohlberg, Inc.

ISBN 0-8114-4078-8 (pbk.)
ISBN 0-8114-2668-8 (lib. bdg.)   LC 89-110888

CONTENTS

1800

SACAJAWEA ▼
She guided Lewis and Clark
into unknown
territory.
(1805–1806)

DANIEL BOONE ▲
His search for wide-open
spaces began the
movement west.
(1769–1775)

◄ **NARCISSA AND**
MARCUS WHITMAN
They were inspired to
travel west, and their
journey inspired others.
(1836)

1850

JOHN FRÉMONT ➤
The Westward Movement
would have stopped short
if not for him.
(1842–1845)

JAMES MARSHALL ➤
His discovery of gold
quickened the race to
the West.
(1844–1848)

◄**WILLIAM RUSSELL**
The thundering hooves of the
Pony Express echoed across
the plains, thanks to him.
(1860–1861)

Daniel Boone

Builder of the
Wilderness Road

It doesn't seem possible. When we first came to North Carolina, I had all the space I needed. Now I feel hemmed in. Hustle and bustle! People! Gone are the wide-open spaces. My eyes keep wandering to the west. I yearn for "elbow room."

DANIEL Boone fumed with anger. He stormed into his little wooden cabin and slammed the door.

"I can't stand it here anymore, Rebecca," he said to his wife. "There are just too many people in North Carolina. I hardly have room to swing my elbows anymore."

Rebecca Boone put down her sewing and looked at her husband. His outburst did not surprise her. Lately he seemed restless all the time.

"Close neighbors are not such a bad thing," Rebecca said softly as she returned to her sewing.

"Close neighbors," said Daniel in a cold voice, "are the thing I hate most in this world. The hunting in this area has been ruined!"

As the weeks went by, Daniel's mood grew worse. He snapped at his children. He growled at Rebecca. And he took little pleasure in hunting or fishing. Finally, on May 1, 1769, he began loading his traveling pack.

"What are you doing?" Rebecca asked in alarm.

"Rebecca, I've decided to travel west and search for a new place to live," he said.

"Where—where are you going?"

"I've been hearing stories about the land out west. 'Kentucky,' they call it. They say the whole area is covered with buffalo, deer, wild turkeys,

and blue-green grass. The soil is so rich that anything will grow there."

"But Daniel, that land is full of Indians!" Rebecca cried, trembling. "It's not safe there."

"Don't worry about me," Daniel replied as he
finished packing. "I can take care of myself. Why,
I can catch a fish with my bare hands. I can build a
shelter with scraps of bark. And I've been shoot-
ing a rifle since I was knee-high. Don't you think I
can handle a few angry Indians?"

"Well—but—" Rebecca paused. "What about
me and the children?"

"I'll come back for you soon," he promised, swinging the pack over his shoulder. "You have enough supplies to last until I return. Our son James will help you with the chores. If you need help, you can call on my brother Squire."

He kissed Rebecca and the children good-bye. Then he headed out into the wilderness toward Kentucky.

Later, when she was alone, Rebecca wondered if she would see her husband again. She understood Daniel's restlessness, but she was worried about his safety.

FOR days, Daniel Boone climbed westward through the Appalachian Mountains with five other men. They moved slowly, picking their way along the rocky ridges. At last they found a break in the mountains. This gap, later named Cumberland Gap, led them into Kentucky.

"Look!" shouted Daniel as he surveyed the land.

"This is spectacular! Look at the trees, the streams, the wide-open spaces! This is what I've been searching for."

The men spent months wandering through Kentucky. By December Daniel's companions were ready to return home to North Carolina. Daniel, however, did not want to leave. He had fallen in love with Kentucky. He decided to stay alone to look for the perfect site for a settlement. He thought often of his family in North Carolina and dreamed of the time when they would all be together again.

One day, soon after his friends departed, Daniel was sitting by a river cleaning his gun. Suddenly he heard a twig crack. He jumped up and ran behind a tree. "Indians," he thought to himself. He felt his muscles tighten and his heart pump wildly. He did not have time to load his gun. He would have to fight the enemy with his bare hands.

Just then, a familiar voice called his name.

Daniel listened. It couldn't be. But it was.

Daniel's brother Squire emerged from the forest.

"Squire!" shouted Daniel, running to greet him. "What are you doing here?"

"Rebecca sent me. She asked me to hunt you down and see if you were still alive."

"Rebecca always did worry too much," Daniel said, laughing. "As you can see, I'm alive and well."

Squire settled into Daniel's camp. He spent a few weeks exploring the fields of Kentucky with

Daniel. Then he packed up his things for the journey home.

"What should I tell Rebecca?" he asked as he left.

"Tell her I'll come back as soon as I've located the perfect spot for our new home," said Daniel. "Give her and the children my love. Tell them that I will keep my promise."

A whole year passed before Daniel was satisfied with his choice of land. At last he returned to North Carolina and his wife and family.

"My dear," he said when he saw Rebecca, "I've come back to take you all to Kentucky. I have found the perfect place to live. It's a beautiful meadow with clear water, plenty of fish and game, great farm land, and, best of all, no other people!"

Daniel's excitement about the new land was contagious. Five neighboring families decided to go with them. And so, in September 1773, the group set out for the beautiful but dangerous land of Kentucky.

The journey was hard. The travelers had to scramble up steep inclines and wind through dense forests. There was no road to follow, so they could not use a wagon. All their possessions were carried in small carts pulled by oxen.

Each family had space to bring only the bare essentials: some pots and pans, a butter churn, and some clothes. The women rode on horses with their children. The men walked alongside them, carrying rifles. At night the men stayed with the women and children. The teenage boys slept nearby, guarding the animals.

"James," Daniel told his sixteen-year-old son. "You boys are in charge of the animals at night. If you hear anything unusual, come get me."

"Don't worry, Pa," said James. "We'll be fine."

For two weeks all went well. Then tragedy struck. Early on the morning of October 10,

Shawnee Indians attacked without warning. They crept up on the sleeping boys and killed them. James never had a chance to call for his father's help. The attack was obviously a warning for the settlers to stay out of Shawnee territory.

The death of her son and the other boys horrified Rebecca. She wept and wept, and could not be comforted. She refused to take another step toward Kentucky. The other families felt the same way. Only Daniel Boone wanted to keep going.

"I loved my son," he told the despairing group. "And I loved the other boys. But the fact is, they are gone now. We cannot change that. All we can do is pledge revenge. And the best way to get revenge is to keep going into Kentucky. White settlers must move in and drive the Indians off the land."

But the families' grief was too great. They no longer wanted to continue the journey. They asked Daniel to take them back to North Carolina. Sadly, he agreed.

BACK in his cabin on the Yadkin River, Daniel lived quietly. He hunted, fished, and farmed. But still he dreamed of living in Kentucky. He wanted his friends and family to try the westward journey again. He knew he first had to find a way to make the trip safer and easier.

BY March 1775, he thought he had the answer. He gathered thirty of the toughest men he knew.

"Men," he said, "I'm going to build a road into Kentucky."

The men stared at him in disbelief.

"Are you crazy?" one demanded. "Why, Kentucky is over 250 miles away. It's on the other side of the Appalachians. It would take you forever!"

"Yes," said Daniel, "it would take forever if I worked alone. That's why I want you to help me. Together we can do it in a month."

"If the Indians don't kill us first," muttered another.

"I know it's risky," Boone admitted. "But when we're finished, I'll give each of you four hundred acres of good Kentucky land for your hard work. We'll make a new American colony there."

The men talked it over and decided to accept the challenge. Bravely they set out. They moved along slowly, cutting a trail wide enough for wagons. They made their way into the mountains.

After about 235 miles, a band of Shawnees spotted them. That night the Indians swooped down. Luckily, most of Daniel's men ran for cover. Only a few were killed. But the attack frightened them. They wanted to quit.

"We can't turn back now," Daniel pleaded with them. "We've come too far. Please, I promise you—if there's any more trouble, we'll go home. But let's give it one more try."

Daniel's promise worked. The men returned to their task. Finally, on April 20, 1775, they reached the other side of the mountains. They had completed the Wilderness Road. Ahead of them flowed the Kentucky River. Beyond that lay the beautiful fields of Kentucky.

"We did it!" cried Daniel joyfully. "We really did it!"

Great dangers remained, of course. Hostile Indians inhabited the land. But white settlers now had a road over the mountains into Kentucky.

That fall, Daniel returned to North Carolina for his family. The frontier was slowly but surely moving westward. Daniel Boone's courage and independent spirit opened the West for thousands of settlers who would follow him.

SACAJAWEA
GUIDE FOR LEWIS AND CLARK

I've known many hardships. As a child, I was kidnapped by Indians of another tribe. I was their captive for years. A French fur trader found me and brought me to his home. I married him and now live here.

But my heart still aches for the members of my tribe. I long to see them… somewhere, some time.

SACAJAWEA sat in her lodge in Fort Mandan, North Dakota. In her arms she held her newborn son, Jean Baptiste, or "Pompey" as she called him.

"I know you don't approve," she said to her friend Issapahki. "But I think I am going to accept Captain Lewis's invitation to go on the journey."

Her friend looked at her in disbelief. "Why would you choose to leave your home and head west with a group of white explorers?"

"Because they need me," replied Sacajawea.

"I don't see how you could be of much help."

Sacajawea shrugged. "Well, Captain Lewis needs someone who can speak the Shoshone language. He and Captain Clark are traveling west all the way to the Pacific Ocean. They told me that President Jefferson wants the expedition to gather information about the unexplored territory purchased from France. I'm the only person they can find who can translate Shoshone."

Sacajawea dropped her voice to a whisper and added, "Actually, Captain Lewis didn't really want to ask me. He thinks a woman will slow the group down. And he's worried about the baby." She looked down at her sleeping infant and smiled.

"Well, what *will* you do with the baby?" asked Issapahki.

"He will come with me. He can ride on my back. My husband is coming, too. Although not an Indian, he knows other Indian languages and can help the expedition."

Issapahki shook her head. "You can't be serious," she said. "Don't you realize how difficult the trip will be? You will be traveling on foot for thousands of miles!"

"Of course I do," said Sacajawea calmly. "But I am no stranger to hardships."

After a pause, she continued. "There's another reason I want to go," she told Issapahki. "I may find Shoshone tribes who can give me news about my family. I have not seen them for years. It's only a small chance. But how happy I would be! It would be worth every hardship."

ON April 7, 1805, the explorers began their journey. About 40 people went, including soldiers, woodsmen, hunters, and traders. For six weeks they traveled up the Missouri River in eight boats. Lewis and Clark wrote daily records in their journals and made maps of the new land.

It was not an easy trip. On cloudless days the sun's rays were so strong that Sacajawea's eyes ached and her head felt swollen. On rainy days she was soaked to her bones. Worst of all was the wind. Strong gusts whipped sand from the riverbank into her face. Her eyes stung and her skin burned. But she did not complain. Rather, she held her head high and worked as hard as the rest. She seemed indifferent to every difficulty.

One night, while the others slept, Captain William Clark woke up and decided to check the area. As he walked around the campsite, he saw Sacajawea sitting under a tree. In the moonlight he could see her rubbing little Pompey's legs.

"Is something wrong?" he asked. "Is he sick?"

"No," said Sacajawea. "He is not sick. I am just rubbing his legs as I do every night. Pompey is wrapped up all day. So at night I need to get the blood moving again."

Clark did not know what to say. Even the strongest men on the trip were exhausted by the end of the day. Yet this amazing young woman stayed up late every night and cheerfully rose every morning with the sun.

As the weeks wore on, the river became wilder and rougher. One day a sharp breeze rose out of nowhere and caught the sail on Sacajawea's boat.

The boat lurched to the side, and icy water rushed in. Bottles of medicine, directional charts, and the compass began tumbling into the water.

"No!" shouted Captain Lewis when he saw these valuables disappearing. Without them, the journey could not continue.

In an instant, Sacajawea sprang into action. Clutching the edge of the boat with one hand, she leaned far out over the rushing water. She grabbed the bottles of medicine as they bobbed by and tossed them over her shoulder into the boat. Then she reached out again and saved the directional charts. Finally, stretching out so far that she

was practically in the water, she plucked the compass from the waves. That, too, she tossed back into the boat.

"I can't believe it!" Lewis cried to Clark as the others broke into applause.

"She's amazing, isn't she?" they whispered to one another.

A few days later, the party crossed a new river. The captains named it Birdwoman's River in honor of Sacajawea, whose name meant "bird woman." She had become the new heroine of their journey.

TWO weeks later, on June 10, the group reached a series of waterfalls that stretched for miles. They were dismayed as they tried to decide what to do.

"Well," said Lewis, "we've got no choice. We can't take the boats over the falls. We'll have to walk for a while."

The walk was steep and hard. The men slowly dragged the boats over land. They were weary, but their valiant guide, Sacajawea, smiled and bravely marched ahead, leading them onward. How could they complain?

What they did not know was that Sacajawea was very sick. She could not eat. Pain shot through her stomach, and fever racked her body.

In time both Lewis and Clark pleaded with her to stop and rest. But she refused.

"I promised that I would not slow you down," she said to them. "And I will keep my promise."

But by the tenth day Sacajawea seemed near death. Captain Lewis announced a halt. He ordered Sacajawea to lie down and made her drink spring water and eat buffalo soup. After two days, she felt stronger and announced that she could go on.

"I am ready to go," she told Captain Lewis. "Please, let the journey continue."

In a few days the group reached the Rocky Mountains. Here the travelers found fewer plants and animals to eat. Lewis and Clark saw they could no longer follow the Missouri River. They needed horses to cross the mountains. The winter snows would begin soon.

"We need horses to get over mountains, but where can we get them?" said Clark. A feeling, not unlike despair, came over the group. They looked at the cold, desolate landscape stretching for miles. They shivered in the cold as they looked toward the mountains.

Suddenly someone spotted a cloud of dust in the distance. As they watched, a group of Indians emerged, riding toward them. Fearfully the group turned toward their Birdwoman who studied the approaching braves. In a moment her face was wreathed in smiles. "They are Shoshone," she called to Lewis and Clark. With her arms outstretched she walked toward them, her baby strapped to her back.

The young warriors were shocked to see an Indian woman, one of their own, in the midst of these foreign men. They slowed to a halt, facing her.

Sacajawea began talking slowly, in a language she had not used for many years. Suddenly she stopped. She stared at the young chief, astonished. Then she burst into tears.

"My brother!" she cried.

Everyone looked at the two of them. It was true! The young Shoshone chief was Cameahwait, Sacajawea's long-lost brother! With tears streaming down his face, he embraced his sister. A wave of emotion swept through the group. Each one knew what it meant to love and lose a brother or sister. Each could share in the joy of these two who had found each other again.

Glowing with great happiness, Sacajawea and Cameahwait talked for hours. Cameahwait told his sister how he had become a chief, and Sacajawea told him about life with the white men.

"These are good people," she told Cameahwait. "And they need your help. Without it, I am afraid they will die this winter."

Cameahwait could not refuse his sister. He gave the explorers the horses they needed. Then he took Sacajawea aside.

"Why don't you stay with us?" he urged her. "Stay here with your family. You do not belong with the white man."

Sacajawea looked at Cameahwait for a long time before responding. When she spoke, her voice was firm but touched with sadness.

"I cannot stay," she said. "These men still have many miles to travel, and need my help. Besides, they have become my family. I cannot desert them. But I will never forget this day, or you, my blood brother. This day is a day like a thousand days; it will shine forever in my heart."

AND so, they parted. For the next fifteen months, Sacajawea would travel with Lewis and Clark. She would walk with them all the way to the Pacific Ocean, and then all the way back to Fort Mandan, North Dakota. During the 8,000 mile journey, she would prove her value to the group again and again.

Her name would live forever in the journals of Lewis and Clark. The story of her strength and endurance would be told over and over again. After her death, memorials would be built in her honor. In fact, to this day, more statues are dedicated to Sacajawea than to any other North American woman.

John Frémont
The Pathfinder

Since I was a boy, I have dreamed of opening up faraway lands and making unknown countries known. I felt that action, adventure, glory, and great deeds waited for me away out yonder under the path of the setting sun.

Now, as I look down on this unexplored valley, it seems as if Nature had collected all her beauties together in one chosen place. The drama, light, and purity of this delightful land beckon me onward, farther west!

OHN Charles Frémont had not slept in a real bed in almost six weeks. He had not read a newspaper or looked in a mirror. Since June 15, 1842, he and the men on his expedition had been traveling through the western wilderness and the great Rocky Mountains. It had been a slow and difficult journey. But that had not dampened Frémont's spirits. In fact, every day he seemed to grow more and more enthusiastic.

"I love this land!" he exclaimed to his guide, Kit Carson, as they stood at the headwaters of the Green River in Wyoming. "There's just one thing I don't understand. Other explorers have come this way. They've passed through the plains and come up into these mountains. Yet they call this region a wasteland. They're wrong! This land is wonderful! It's—it's magnificent! Why didn't they see that?"

"I don't know," said Carson with a shrug.

Indeed, other explorers had labeled the plains "The Great American Desert." They had declared the area unfit for settlement because it did not appear suitable for farming and was inhabited by Indian tribes.

Frémont saw things differently. When he stood on the plains, he felt refreshed by the cool dry winds. When he knelt on the banks of Nebraska's Platte River, he felt the excitement of the rushing water. And when he climbed into the Rockies, he felt the staggering power of their rugged heights. He was inspired by the beauty that he saw. He was also inspired by the secret purpose of his trip.

Frémont's father-in-law, the powerful Senator Thomas Hart Benton, had convinced Congress to fund this trip and to make Frémont its leader.

The goal of the trip was to survey the Oregon Trail and map the West. But for Benton and his supporters, the trip had a second, even more important purpose. They wanted the United States to expand westward to the Pacific Ocean. They wanted settlers to move west. Frémont's secret mission was to show that the West was a suitable place for settlement. Benton and others hoped that Americans would decide to move west once they learned of the benefits of this vast area.

Frémont enjoyed his mission. He did indeed see the land as beautiful. In his journal he jotted down enchanting descriptions of what he saw. In his mind he was already writing the report of his trip. He pictured himself as a romantic, bold adventurer who was exploring beautiful, unknown lands.

FRÉMONT turned to his friend. "One day, Kit, one day all this land will be settled. Ranches and farms and towns will stretch all the way to this river."

"Now how do you figure that?" Kit laughed. "Your own men don't even want to be here."

Frémont glanced at his 25 followers. They sat resting on rocks, looking tired and bored.

"Hmmm," Frémont thought to himself. "The men *do* look worn out." He pondered this fact for a minute. Then his face lit up with the fresh excitement of a new idea.

"What the men need," he thought to himself, "is inspiration. They need someone to remind them of the importance of this journey for our country. And I think I have the perfect plan for doing that."

For the next few days, Frémont pushed his men through the craggy Wind River Mountain Range. Finally he found what he was looking for.

"Men," he announced, "take a look at that."

Frémont stretched out his arm and pointed to a mountain that loomed in front of them.

"That is the highest peak in the Rockies," he proclaimed. "And we are going to climb it."

"How do you know it's the highest?" one of the men called out.

"And why do we have to climb it?" asked another.

In truth, Frémont was not sure it was the highest peak. But it was the highest one in the area. That was good enough for him.

"Just follow me," he commanded.

Grudgingly, the men followed Frémont's order. When at last they reached the summit, Frémont reached into his pack and pulled out an American flag and a small pole. After fastening the flag to the pole, he stuck it into a crack in the rock.

"I hereby claim this land for the United States of America!" he shouted.

It was a grand gesture, and the men suddenly felt their spirits lift. As the flag unfurled, everyone shouted, "Hurrah!" They felt swept up in the historic event. Their efforts took on new meaning as they imagined this flag towering over all of the Rocky Mountains. Every time they thought about the flag flying on top of that mountain, they remembered the importance of their journey.

"We are part of history now," said one man, beaming with pride. The rest of the men felt it, too. Some nodded in agreement.

WHEN the group finally returned to Kansas City, Frémont thanked all of them for their help. Then he left for Washington, D.C., to join his family and report his findings.

Senator Benton was pleased with Frémont's glowing descriptions of the journey. "I just hope your written account is as exciting as your stories are," he remarked.

FRÉMONT began work. With the help of his wife, Jessie, he wrote over 200 pages describing the trip.

The report was as sparkling and full of excitement as Frémont himself. It described the scenery of the West in glowing terms. It gave dazzling descriptions of the valleys, rivers, and animals. It also told pioneers where they could find good campsites with plenty of grass and water.

His report made the readers feel as if they were on the expedition with him:

> The air at sunrise is clear and pure, and the morning extremely cold, but beautiful. A lofty snow peak of the mountain is glittering in the first rays of the sun. The long mountain wall to the east, rising two thousand feet abruptly from

the plain, is still dark, and cuts clear against the glowing sky. The scenery becomes hourly more interesting and grand, and the view here is truly magnificent. The sun has just shot above the wall, and makes a magical change. The whole valley is glowing and bright, and all the mountain peaks are gleaming like silver.

True to his vision, Frémont portrayed himself as a bold adventurer. The report ended with a dramatic description of his climb up the mountain to plant the flag on the peak:

I sprang upon the summit, and another step would have precipitated me into an immense snow field five hundred feet below. To the edge of this field was a sheer icy precipice; and then, with a gradual fall, the field sloped off for about a mile. I stood on a narrow crest, about three feet in width, and, fixing a ramrod in a crevice, unfurled the national flag to wave in the breeze where never flag waved before…. We had climbed the loftiest peak of the Rocky Mountains, and, standing where never human foot had stood before, felt the exultation of first explorers.

"I think the public will love this report," Frémont said to his wife.

And he was right. When the government published the report, people were enchanted by it. They began to change their opinion of the West.

Quickly John Frémont became a popular romantic hero. He was nicknamed "The Pathfinder" in honor of his exploration. Congress even approved a second trip for him. He was asked to go all the way to the Columbia River in the Oregon Territory.

FRÉMONT felt more excited than ever. In May 1843, he went to St. Louis, Missouri, and recruited 40 men to go with him. The group set out on a new expedition. In November, he and his men reached Oregon. At that point, he was supposed to turn around and head back east. But Frémont could not resist the chance to explore California. So he led his men south toward the Sierra Mountains.

"I don't like this," Carson said in a disapproving voice. "You're disobeying the orders for this expedition."

"Not really," said Frémont with a smile. "I'm not disobeying orders—I'm just stretching them a little."

As the group headed into the Sierras, Frémont's confidence and optimism were sorely tested. Winter proved to be a terrible time to travel through the mountains. Blizzards came often, and huge snowdrifts blocked all paths. Frémont and his men soon ran out of food and were forced to eat their horses to survive. After countless times of being lost, Frémont finally managed to lead his men out of the mountains and returned to complete his report.

When Frémont and his wife wrote the report of this trip, they did not tell of the difficulties. Once again, the West was described as pleasant and inviting. "It is a garden spot," he wrote. Like the first report, this account received wild praise from the public. Frémont was again a hero in the eyes of the people.

In the summer of 1845, "The Pathfinder" set out on yet a third expedition to the West. This time the government asked him to map northern Nevada and the dangerous passes of the Sierra Mountains.

After his return from this latest trip, Frémont observed that Americans began flooding into the West. He was overcome with joy and excitement.

"I'm proud to be part of this great country," he told Jessie. "And I'm proud that I helped make the wonderful western lands part of America."

NARCISSA AND MARCUS WHITMAN

PIONEER MISSIONARIES

I've always been a little different, I know. Young girls my age look forward to marrying a nice young man. And soon there's a home and children.

But for some reason, I feel called to a different life. I long for faraway places. Not just for the adventure. I want to bring something noble and good to less fortunate people!

N ARCISSA Prentiss's heart sank as she read the letter.

"They turned me down!" she cried out loud. "I can't believe it. They actually turned me down!"

Narcissa's mother heard her cries and hurried to her. "What is it, dear?" she asked.

"The Board turned me down. They won't approve my request to begin a mission in the Oregon Territory," said Narcissa.

"Did they say why?" asked her mother.

"They say that they don't accept single women as missionaries."

Mrs. Prentiss sighed. She could understand Narcissa's disappointment. For many years her daughter had wanted to work among the Indians

and spread the Christian religion. But secretly Mrs. Prentiss was relieved. She didn't want her beautiful 26-year-old daughter to head out into the dangerous wilderness. She wanted her to remain close to home.

A short time later, Narcissa met a young doctor, Marcus Whitman. Like Narcissa, Marcus had a burning desire to become a missionary. The two fell in love and became engaged.

"Once we are married, I know the Board will approve us as missionaries," declared Marcus excitedly. "Then we can go out west together and bring Christianity to the Indians."

The next letter that arrived from the Board caused Narcissa to weep again, but these were tears of happiness. She and her husband had been accepted as missionaries.

Narcissa's family, however, was not happy.

"You have no idea what your life will be like, Narcissa," Mrs. Prentiss said. "You don't realize how hard it will be, how lonely. You don't know what dangers await you. You are giving up every-thing for a life of uncertainty and hardship."

"Mother, you know I have dreamed of becom-ing a missionary since I was sixteen years old. And now, at last, I have a chance. Nothing can stop me and no one can talk me out of it."

Mrs. Prentiss did not say another word. But at Narcissa's wedding, she wore black. So did all the female members of the Prentiss family. In their grim mourning clothes, they sobbed throughout the ceremony. Since Narcissa and Marcus would soon leave for the Oregon Territory, their families knew they might never see them again.

"Are you very nervous about our trip west?" Marcus asked Narcissa one day shortly after their wedding. "After all, no white woman has ever crossed the Rocky Mountains."

Narcissa shook her head. "Absolutely not," she said. "I am anxious to begin our mission."

IN the spring of 1836, Marcus and Narcissa left New York and headed west. In Cincinnati, they met Henry and Eliza Spalding, a young missionary couple who would go with them. As the group set out over the plains, they said good-bye to a comfortable, familiar way of life and discovered what a difficult journey they faced.

"I'm so tired," complained Eliza after several days on horseback. "And I'm so sore I can hardly move."

None of them were used to the rough edges of frontier life. And without a guide, they weren't even sure how to get to the Oregon Territory.

Luckily, they met some fur traders who were

headed for the Rocky Mountains. The missionaries introduced themselves, and Marcus asked if his small group could travel with them.

"Ordinarily, I'd say no," said the traders' leader bluntly. "But you say you're a doctor. We sure could use a doctor. Never know when one of us might take an arrow."

The trader laughed heartily. But Narcissa was horrified at the thought.

"Was he serious?" she asked Marcus later.

"About the arrow? I'm afraid so. The Indians and the traders don't always get along well."

Narcissa shuddered. But she did not want to show her fear, so she said nothing.

The further west they traveled, the more diffi-cult the journey became. As they moved through the prairie, wood became impossible to find. So instead, they used buffalo chips to build fires. Worse yet, their supplies were dwindling.

"Marcus, look how little flour we have left. Soon we won't be able to bake bread. What will we eat?" Narcissa asked anxiously.

"Don't worry, dear. Look at all those buffalo," he replied. "We may get tired of eating just one thing, but we won't starve."

THE little party traveled many days across the windswept plains. The scenery never seemed to change and Narcissa wondered if they were moving at all. Then one afternoon, she saw something coming toward them on the horizon. Finally she could make out a small group of trav-elers. They were riding east—toward home! She could send a letter home! She hurried to get paper and pen. She made ink by adding water to violet powder.

Narcissa wrote as fast as she could. She wanted to tell about the sights she had seen and her new frontier life. But all too soon, she had to finish with a hasty "Farewell," and give her letter to the travelers. Momentarily, she was filled with long-ing for her family and friends so far away.

She missed them so. But as she turned to survey the vast land before her, she was not sorry for her decision. Although the trip was difficult, she was looking forward to their final destination — a mission of their own.

As they continued, the countryside finally changed. The prairies became hills. Then the hills became mountains. As Narcissa looked at the Rocky Mountains rising before her, she knew the most difficult part of the trip lay ahead. Hauling the wagon over the treacherous paths became a major task. The narrow, rocky trails led over high passes and into deep canyons. Many times Narcissa clung to the saddle, terrified, as her horse picked its way along the side of a steep mountain.

If one hoof slipped, she could be sent tumbling to the jagged rocks 500 feet below the trail.

Each evening, she felt exhausted from the hard day's travels. After several weeks of this strenuous routine, Narcissa felt as if she could not continue.

"Maybe we could stop for a few days and rest," she suggested at last. She felt tired and weak, and she knew that Eliza was feeling even worse.

"I'm sorry, but we can't," Marcus said gently. "We've got to push on ahead. We must reach the Columbia River before winter hits."

Narcissa resolved not to complain again. She refreshed herself with the beauty that surrounded them. In her journal she described the strangely shaped rock formations, the abundant wildflowers, the fresh scent of the pines, and the sunsets over the snow-capped peaks.

UNFORTUNATELY, their troubles were not over. As they traveled over the Rockies, their food supply dwindled. The fur traders headed off higher into the mountains to conduct their business with the trappers. The Whitmans and the Spaldings were left to fend for themselves. Before long, they ran out of dried buffalo meat. They had to live on wild berries and whatever plants they could find.

"I don't think we're going to make it," Henry Spalding declared one night as the four of them huddled around a small fire. "We'll never find our way out of these mountains."

Panic and despair settled over the group. But Narcissa refused to sink into depression. After a few minutes of silence, she stood up and began singing a hymn. Her clear, crisp voice echoed through the mountains, raising the spirits of her companions.

Marcus looked at her with admiration. "If anyone can make it across these mountains," he proclaimed, "we can."

After several more days of traveling, the four missionaries finally began working their way out of the mountains.

"We're almost there," cried Narcissa. "I can feel it."

As they came down from the mountains, they found more food—all kinds of game. Their spirits rose, and they hurried toward their destination.

Late one afternoon, they climbed a ridge. Below them stretched the shining Columbia River.

"Marcus! Look! We're here! We've finally arrived!" Narcissa exclaimed in awe.

"Praise be! After six long months, we have reached the Promised Land!" Marcus replied.

THE Whitmans set up their mission among the Cayuse Indians. The mission was near what is today Walla Walla, Washington. They named it Waiilatpu—the place of rye grass.

One day a messenger brought exciting news. A group of twenty settlers was traveling toward the mission. Narcissa hurried to prepare a large meal, while Marcus readied his medical supplies. The Whitmans greeted the settlers warmly.

"How was your trip?" Narcissa asked one of the women.

"It was more difficult than I ever imagined," the woman replied. "But because of you and your husband, we knew it could be done. That thought gave us the encouragement and confidence to keep going. Whenever we felt discouraged, we would think of you and the mission waiting here for us. I admire your courage, Mrs. Whitman. By daring to go first, you opened the way west for all pioneer women."

JAMES MARSHALL
FIRST TO FIND GOLD

Finally the sawmill is ready. The workers want to begin. In a short time, I'll be a success! And that's why I came all the way from New Jersey to California.

But what is that in the water? Yellow and shiny. Could it be gold? If it is, what does that mean — for me, for my sawmill and dreams of success?

J AMES Marshall left New Jersey looking for a new and exciting place to settle. He wanted a place with opportunities — a place where he could test his talents, prove his courage, and get rich. He drifted farther and farther west.

"Perhaps California is where I will make my fortune," he thought. In 1844, Marshall joined a wagon train bound for the West Coast. When he finally reached California, he decided to stay in Sutter's Fort, which later became Sacramento. There he met John Sutter, the man who had founded the settlement.

"I need a job. Any chance you're looking for a new employee?" Marshall asked Sutter.

"What are your skills, young man?" replied Sutter.

"I am a wheelwright and carpenter. I'm a hard worker and can do any task you give me," Marshall answered confidently.

"I just may have something for you to do," commented Sutter as he looked over this bold young stranger.

"I should let you know, though," Marshall continued, "I intend to make my life a success. Whatever job I take must help me reach my goal."

Sutter nodded. "I like a man with ambition. What do you know about the lumber business?"

"Everything a man might need to know," said Marshall as he thought back to the summer he built his own home. "Building a home is part of the lumber business," he thought to himself.

"Good," said Sutter. "I need a large supply of lumber to run my ranch. The only way I can get enough is to open my own sawmill. How would you like to be my partner?" asked Sutter.

"Partner!" exclaimed Marshall. "What would my job be?"

"You would be in charge of the sawmill. You would oversee its construction. Then when the mill is finished, you would manage its day-to-day operation. I will pay for the construction costs.

Once we begin producing lumber, we'll share the profits," answered Sutter.

Marshall closed his eyes for a minute. "Yes," he thought, "I can picture myself running a saw-mill." He could almost hear the whir of the saw blades and smell the aroma of freshly cut pine boards. He could see himself as a man of power and prestige among the workers.

"All right," he said at last. He grasped Sutter's hand in a firm handshake. "It's a deal."

IN the summer of 1847, Marshall traveled 50 miles east to the site of the new sawmill. The first thing he did was to meet with the Coloma Indians. He offered them a fair price for the land where the sawmill would be built. The Coloma appreciated Marshall's fairness and accepted his

offer. From that time forward, Marshall had a good relationship with the Indians.

It took several long months to build the sawmill. But at last, it was finished. By January 23, 1848, only one task remained. Someone had to dig a little more dirt out of the tailrace. This ditch led water away from the waterwheel. It was important to the mill's smooth operation.

"Well," thought Marshall, "I'll get up early and do it myself. By tomorrow evening, we'll be in business."

The next morning, Marshall awoke at dawn and headed down toward the waterwheel. When he reached the tailrace, something caught his eye — something shining in the water.

Marshall stared at the glistening object in amazement. He had never seen anything like it. Carefully he picked the nugget up. As he studied it, one thought kept dancing through his brain: could this be gold?

"It couldn't be...," he whispered. "Or could it?"

He wanted to be certain. He pulled a gold coin from his pocket. The nugget was the same color as the coin. Next Marshall set the nugget down and pounded it with a rock. Most rocks or metals would have shattered. But the nugget simply flattened out.

Marshall became even more excited. He rushed back to his room, holding the sparkling metal carefully in the palm of his hand. He found some lye, the strong substance used for making soap, and poured it into a pot. He set the pot over the fire in the fireplace. When the lye was boiling, he dropped the nugget into the pot.

"This should settle it," he thought anxiously. "If it isn't gold, it will melt or crack or burn."

But the nugget did not melt. It did not crack or burn. When Marshall completed this last test, he felt certain of his discovery.

"Gold!" he whispered gleefully. "I've found gold! Gold! Gold! Gold!"

MARSHALL could not wait to share the good news with his partner. He wrote a note to his workers telling them to open the sawmill. Then he jumped on his horse and galloped off toward Sutter's Fort. In his pocket, wrapped in a clean handkerchief, was the precious yellow nugget he had taken from the tailrace.

When Marshall had gone just a few miles, he ran into a terrible rainstorm. But that didn't stop him. On he rode, hardly noticing the cold rain that soaked his clothes. He arrived at Sutter's home, drenched with water and splattered with mud. He pounded on the front door.

"For heaven's sake," exclaimed Sutter as he opened the door. When he saw his wild-eyed partner, he stared at him with concern. "James! What's wrong? Why aren't you at the sawmill?"

"I can't tell you here," cried Marshall breathlessly. "Someone might hear me. Once we're behind locked doors, I'll explain everything."

Sutter continued to stare at Marshall. "Have you gone crazy?" he asked after a minute. "What is the problem?"

"I can't tell you out here. Please," Marshall urged, "please, let's go someplace private."

Sutter motioned Marshall inside. He led him into his study and closed the door. Marshall stood there, dripping wet. He reached into his pocket and pulled out the handkerchief that held the yellow ore.

"Take a look at this," he said, unwrapping the nugget and holding it out to Sutter. "I found this in the tailrace this morning."

Sutter looked bewildered for a moment. Then his expression changed. His eyes grew wide and his mouth dropped open.

"Is this what I think it is?"

"You bet," Marshall exclaimed with a broad grin. "It's gold!"

"Are you sure?" Sutter asked.

MARSHALL described the tests he had conducted. Sutter listened intently, then he went over to the bookshelf and pulled out an encyclopedia. Sutter read aloud about all the qualities and properties of gold. As one final test, he dipped the nugget in nitric acid. The nugget did not change. Sutter was convinced. It was gold!

Sutter sighed and ran his hands over his eyes. Gold …

"Isn't this fantastic?" Marshall said, bubbling with excitement.

"No!" snapped Sutter abruptly. "No, James! Don't you see? This will ruin us!"

"What are you talking about?" cried Marshall. "It's a dream come true."

"Sooner or later this news is going to get out. And then we'll have gold diggers crawling all over our land. Our workers will run off to look for gold, and we'll have to shut down the mill. Gold will be disastrous for us. The Indians have a legend about gold. They say that whoever finds gold will have bad luck."

Marshall did not believe a word of this. He laughed and told Sutter to stop worrying. But six months later, Marshall was no longer laughing. Word of his discovery had leaked out. Miners flocked to his land. They set up campsites all around Sutter's sawmill. Everyone ignored Marshall's attempt to protect his territory. Sutter and Marshall were forced to give up their claim to the land.

Sutter's predictions were coming true. The workers at the sawmill deserted their posts. They, too, went off into the hills in search of gold. Marshall was left with a beautiful new sawmill and no one to help run it. All of his hopes for great fortunes were disappearing.

Relations with the Coloma Indians worsened in a hurry. The gold diggers did not respect any of the tribe's rights. The Indians felt threatened by the large numbers of men arriving each week. Hostility and bloodshed broke out between the Indians and the miners.

THROUGHOUT 1848, Marshall watched helplessly as his hopes for success crumbled around him. Without help to run the sawmill, he and Sutter were forced to close it.

For a while Marshall joined the other gold diggers. Some of the miners thought Marshall had magic power to find gold. One time a group of rowdy men threatened to hang him if he didn't lead them to gold.

Other than that first nugget, however, Marshall did not have luck finding gold. He never found more than a few ounces.

Marshall recalled the Indian legend Sutter had told him. He wondered when his bad luck would end.

WILLIAM RUSSELL
FOUNDER OF THE PONY EXPRESS

 Mr. Russell, I hear you are looking for young men. If you need a good rider who isn't afraid of long trips, I hope you'll take me. I can outride any Indian, and I don't mind bad weather or lonely places. If you provide fast horses and food and lodging, I'm ready to go!

W ANTED: Young, skinny, wiry fellows, not over eighteen. Must be expert riders, willing to risk death daily. Orphans preferred."

William Hepburn Russell printed these words on posters in March of 1860. Then he tacked the posters up all around St. Joseph, Missouri.

Ben Holladay, a friend of Russell's, spied him putting up a poster.

"What are you up to now?" quizzed Holladay.

Russell smiled. "I'm starting a new mail service. It's going to run all the way to Sacramento, California."

"Why would you want to do that?" questioned Holladay. "We've already got mail service to California."

"Yes, but stagecoaches take four weeks to reach Sacramento. Pack mules take even longer. My service is going to be faster. I'm going to get mail from here to Sacramento in ten days."

"Can't be done," said Holladay flatly.

"Yes, it can," Russell countered.

"Yeah? How are you going to manage it?"

"With horses!" Russell declared. "Call it a horse express. Or better yet, a Pony Express!"

Holladay shook his head and walked away. "I don't know," he called over his shoulder. "I'll believe it when I see it."

Holladay was not the only one who doubted Russell's idea. Many people shook their heads in disbelief. Russell had experience building a successful freight company. It handled the movement of supplies all over the United States. Yet in this particular venture, even his business partners, Alexander Majors and Bill Waddell, expressed their doubts when they met together.

"What worries me is the time deadline," said Waddell. "Ten days just isn't long enough."

"Listen," said Russell, "I have it all figured out. We'll hire about 80 riders. Each rider will cover about 75 miles. There will be new horses waiting at stations every 15 miles. If the riders go nonstop, they can make it."

"I'm not worried about the time," Majors declared. "I'm thinking about the Indians. These riders will be riding alone through the most desolate land there is. Sure, we'll have stations every fifteen miles. But even the stations will be targets for Indian attacks."

When Majors finished speaking, Russell stood up. "Look," he said, "I know it's risky. But 30 riders have already signed up to work for me. *They're* willing to take the risks. I think we should be, too."

With that, Russell strode out of the room. He didn't want to hear any more arguments against his plan.

All through the month of March, Russell tended to details. He checked on the stations being built in Kansas, Nebraska, Wyoming, Utah, and Nevada. He hired station keepers for all 157 stations. He stocked the stations with food and supplies. Finally, he bought 400 small but sturdy horses. In all, he spent over $100,000 setting up the Pony Express.

O N April 3, 1860, the Pony Express was ready to go. Russell ordered one sack of mail to be sent eastward from Sacramento, California. He ordered another sack to be sent westward from St. Joseph, Missouri.

Late that afternoon, Russell walked to downtown St. Joseph. He found Billy Richardson waiting for him. Richardson would be the first man in the long chain of westward riders.

"Well, son," said Russell, "this is it. Are you all set?"

"Just say the word," said Richardson, "and I'm on my way."

"Do you have everything you need? You've got your knife?"

"Yes, sir."

"And your two revolvers?"

"Yes, sir."

"Your spurs and your quirt?"

"Yes."

"Good. Now all you need is your mail."

The mail was due in at 5:00 P.M. on a train from the East. But the mail train was two hours late.

When it finally rolled in, Richardson grabbed the westbound sack of 82 letters. Then he jumped onto his waiting mare.

"Good luck, my boy," said Russell, reaching up and shaking Richardson's hand.

"Thank you, Mr. Russell. And don't worry: I'll get the mail through."

With that, Richardson galloped off. Along the streets of St. Joseph, a crowd of people cheered him on. But as he left the town, he headed into the dark spring night alone.

"I'm already two hours behind schedule," he mumbled anxiously to himself.

About an hour later, Richardson galloped into the first station. He jumped onto a fresh horse. He did the same at the next two stations. During his whole ride, he pushed his ponies to run faster, always faster.

At last he galloped into the town of Seneca, Kansas. A new rider grabbed the mail sack and took off. Exhausted, Richardson checked into the Smith Hotel and fell asleep.

FOR the next nine days, rider after rider charged westward with the precious mail sack. Some riders managed to shave time off their routes. Others ran into unexpected trouble. Henry Wallace hit mud so deep that his horse could barely wade through it. Thomas King ran into such a fierce thunderstorm that his mustang panicked. As the horse reared, the mail sack came loose and sailed over a cliff. King had to scramble down and retrieve it before he could continue.

After six days, the westbound mail was eighteen hours behind schedule. The eastbound riders were also having problems. Warren Upson had to cross the Sierra Mountains during a raging blizzard. Snow made the tiny trail impossible to follow. Upson had to dismount and lead his horse up the steep, rocky cliffs. At times he struggled through snowdrifts thirty feet high.

Another rider, "Ras" Egan, had to cross a river swollen by heavy rains. The swift current knocked the horse off its feet. The poor animal was swept downstream into a bed of quicksand. Egan knew he had to make a quick decision.

"If I take the time to get this horse free, I'll never make my deadline," he thought frantically to himself.

With a lump in his throat, he gave the sinking horse a final pat. Then he grabbed the mail bag and swam toward the shore. Later, as he hurried down the trail on foot, he spotted a horse and rider. Egan shouted for help. When the stranger heard that Egan was with the Pony Express, he dismounted.

"Here, take my horse," the stranger said, "and good luck to you."

Egan tipped his hat, jumped on the horse, then thundered off. Every muscle in his body strained as he pushed to make up for lost time.

All this time, William Russell sat waiting and worrying in St. Joseph. Every day he became more anxious. At last, April 13 arrived. Russell went to the outskirts of town and scanned the horizon for signs of a rider. The people of St. Joseph crowded the downtown area. In Sacramento, too, citizens poured into the streets. Everyone wanted to see if the Pony Express would meet its deadline. For hours they waited.

Then, just as dusk fell, a rider came storming into St. Joseph. At about the same time in the west, another rider charged into Sacramento.

They had done it! The riders had delivered the mail in just nine days and twenty-two hours—two hours earlier than their deadline. Russell shouted for joy.

THE entire nation cheered the Pony Express and its creator, William Russell. For the next eighteen months, Russell's Pony Express served the citizens of the American West. Eighty brave young boys rode for the company. They rode through floods, ice storms, and blizzards. They rode through blazing midday heat and black starless nights. They even rode through buffalo stampedes. The bad weather and wild animals didn't seem to bother them.

But the Indians did.

"I've got to admit, it makes a man nervous," said one rider, "Pony Bob" Haslam. "You know Indians are out there. You just don't know where they are or when they'll attack."

One day, Haslam's fears came true. He was riding through a lonely stretch of Nevada desert. Suddenly, he found himself surrounded by Paiute Indians. With a bold yell, he dug his heels into his pony's side and charged through the hostile braves. As he rode, bullets flew around him. He felt a bullet hit him in the jaw. Then others lodged in his arm. Haslam kept riding. He managed to make it to a station before he collapsed.

Despite the danger, the riders of the Pony Express loved their job. They thrilled to the challenge, and even more, they reveled in the attention. Many of the riders became local heroes.

Johnnie Frye, for example, was a handsome young rider who won the hearts of many women along his route. They cheered for him and gave him cakes and cookies. One woman invented the doughnut just for Frye. He could spear it on his finger as he rushed by.

E VERYONE thinks the Pony Express is a big success," Russell confided to his old friend Ben Holladay in the spring of 1861. "But there's something they don't know."

"What's that?" asked Holladay.

"It's not making any money. In fact, my partners and I have lost over $200,000."

There was another problem, as well. Telegraph lines were moving west. By October of 1861, new wires stretched from St. Joseph to Sacramento. Instead of ten days, a message could now be sent in minutes. And so, on October 26, 1861, Russell's riders made their final run. They had delivered 34,753 pieces of mail. After just eighteen months, the Pony Express went out of business.

"I know the Pony Express didn't last long," remarked William Russell to his friend Ben Holladay. "But wasn't it great while it lasted?"

"I reckon so," said Holladay. "I reckon so."

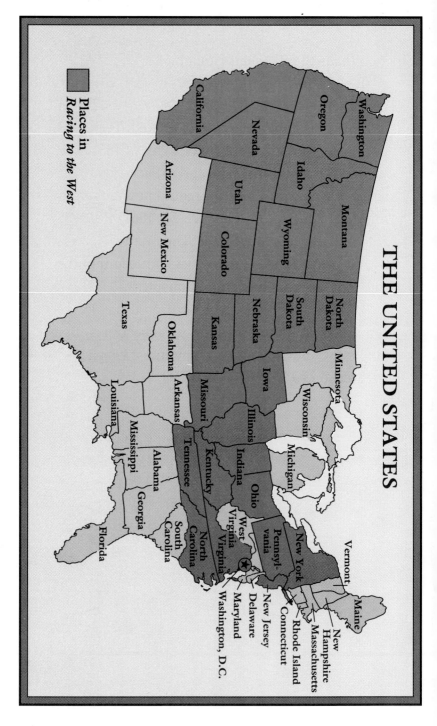

THE UNITED STATES

Places in
Racing to the West